# The Ultimate Desktop Publishing Book

Bill Rosoman Dip CS


Bill Rosoman leftfieldnz@gmail.com

Published by
Bill Rosoman Dip CS

layout and Design by www.lulu.com

Printed by www.lulu.com

Copies of this book can be ordered from
www.lulu.com/leftfieldnz

or
Bill Rosoman
PO Box 4155
Hamilton East 3247
New Zealand

ISBN 978-0-473-17409-5

# The Ultimate Desktop Publishing Book

**Desktop Publishing** using Free Open Source Software. A Brilliant Book giving You All the Tools and Examples You Need to Create That Masterpiece within You.

Creating and publishing a magazine, ezines, books, ebooks, posters, flyers, calendar, menu, certificates, or business cards could Never Be Easier.

## Table of Contents

FOSS or Free Open Source Software is available for most requirements.

## About the Author

I lived and worked for Post Office/Telecom and then myself on the East Coast, above Gisborne, of the North Island of New Zealand for 29 years.

From 2002 to the present I am working, and living in a Campervan, in the Hamilton/Waikato Region of New Zealand with many trips in the region and the North Island.

I have a great interest in Computers and Technology and from that Writing and Publishing Books. This Book "The Ultimate Desktop Publishing Book", is an effort to bring together all my thoughts and writings about using Technology and Computers to Publish Information.

It certainly keeps the brain active and it is great that a lot of free open source software is community supported.

Bill Rosoman Dip CS

July 2010

## Disclaimer

The author, publisher and distributors of this book will in no manner whatsoever assume any responsibility, or liability of any kind for advice or methods provided in this book and used by the reader of this book. The reader assumes all responsibility and liability for his or her actions, as a result of reading this book and using ideas found herein.

In a number of places advice and/or recommendations are given regarding particular companies and their services, and I would like to state that I am in no way employed by any of the companies or services being recommended or suggested, or being paid any fees of any kind for mentioning these companies and their services.

No warranties or guarantees of any kind are being made or implied by the author or publisher as to the reliability or soundness of any of these companies or services being mentioned or recommended. No liability of any kind whatsoever is or will be assumed by the author or publisher.



**Table 1: Important key combinations**

| Function | Key combination | Function | Key combination |
|---|---|---|---|
| Create new file | Ctrl+N | Group objects | Ctrl+G |
| Open file | Ctrl+O | Ungroup objects | Ctrl+U |
| Close file | Ctrl+W | Zoom: Whole page | Ctrl+0 |
| Save file | Ctrl+S | Zoom: Original size | Ctrl+1 |
| File information | Ctrl+I | Soft separation | Ctrl+- |
| Print file | Ctrl+P | Paragraph left justified | Ctrl+L |
| Quit program | Ctrl+Q | Paragraph right justified | Ctrl+R |
| Select all | Ctrl+A | Paragraph centred | Ctrl+E |
| Modifies object | Ctrl+M | Insert page number | Alt+# |
| Duplicate object | Ctrl+D | | |

## Basic Commands

To make things a lot quicker using various Programs it is easy using a few of the Shortcut Keys and Just in Case You Forgot a few;

| | | |
|---|---|---|
| CTRL+C | | Copy |
| CTRL+V | | Paste |
| CTRL+X | | Cut |
| CTRL+P | | Print |
| CTRL+S | | Save |
| CTRL+O | | Open |
| CTRL+B | | Bold |
| CTRL+U | | Underline |
| CTRL+N | | New File |
| CTRL+E | | Center |
| CTRL+A | | Select All |
| CTRL+R | | Replace |
| | | Scribus Shortcuts |
| F5 | | Reload/refresh or Go to a Page |
| F2 | | Rename |
| F3 | or CTRL+F | Find |

| | |
|---|---|
| F7 | Spell Check |
| HOME | Beginning of line |
| CTRL+HOME | Beginning of file |
| END | End of Line |
| CTRL+END | End of File |
| DEL | Delete |
| ALT+F4 | Exit Program |
| ALT+F1 | Menu |
| F12 | Bullets |
| | |
| Home | Beginning of Row |
| End | End of Row |
| Ctrl+Home | Beginning of File |
| Ctrl+End | End of File |
| Del | Delete Highlighted |
| Insert type | Toggle between Insert and Over |
| Page Up | Up One Screen |
| Page Down | Down One Screen |
| Caps Lock | Capitals |
| Shift+Key | Capital or alternative Key |

These are the Basic Command Short Cuts and should work in most programs, of Cause you can go File > Save with you mouse but the Keyboard Short Cuts are so much easier and better on the hands.

We have to remember though that Scribus in particular does follow a lot of the Conventions.
A It is not a Wordprocessor Program Use Open Office for that, or MS Office.
B Scribus does not store much in the file itself, it is just a shell and you need to be careful when moving the file to another folder or computer.

Follow the Instructions for Saving all the Information for Scribus in the Introduction.

## Introduction

This Book is to give you the Technical Skills to Create and Publish. If you would like to learn more about the Technicalities of Writing, I suggest Craig Lock's Book, "How to Write a Book and Get Published".

Available at www.lulu.com/craiglock

Lets get the First Rules of Computing over and done with.

First: Create a Document or Graphic and then save it

straight away and then often.

Second: Save different versions over time so if you do loose everything or if you make a major error you can go back a version Book1.sla then book2.sla etc.

Third: Keep a backup on CD, Flash Drive etc. and do often.

Fourth: Scribus does a good backup if you create an empty folder and the Use File > Collect For Output > Select the Folder > Click on Compress Files and Include Fonts > Click OK.

Fifth: Have Fun Out There!!!!!!!!!!!

Sixth: It is no use cussing and swearing if your computer dies, gets stolen or a file gets corrupted etc. Save and Backup Often.

As with all things in Life, well most of them we need a Plan.

Usually I say you start at the End, IE what are you trying to Achieve and then Plan from there.

I have included some examples of how to create things later in the book.

Doing Your Own Desktop Publishing and Printing could never be easier than it is today and all the Software and Ideas are Free to use, You just need some Knowledge, Time, Inspiration and the Right Tools.

In an era where time and money are scarce commodities maybe its time You Investigated bringing Your Desktop Publishing and Publicity Requirements back In-House.

Using Free Open Source Software FOSS. We have;
Open Office: Wordprocessor etc. Gimp: Graphics and Pictures, Inkscape: Vector Graphics, Calibre: E-Book Reader and Converter, Scribus: Desktop Publishing, Ghostscript: Postscript Stuff, LittleCMS: Colour Management System

All the Software is Cross Platform (Windows, Linux, Apple Mac) and is Free and Legal.

With this Suite of Free Software and some Knowledge and Understanding of Desktop Publishing You have all the Tools You Need to in no t ime Generate all Your In-House Documentation, Advertising and Publicity Material Yourself.

Desktop Publishing can be Fantastic, Professional and Cheap for Most SME Businesses with just a few Tools and some Knowledge and Inspiration.

You will Quickly have Your Masterpiece Ready for In-House Printing or Emailing to Your Friendly Printer.

These Tools will also Future Proof Your Business as all the Tools can be Used across Media, whether it be Print, TV, or Online (The Internet) and on Mobile Devices like Cell Phones and Ipad.

One of the Amazing Features is Making Smart PDF Forms, that Customers can Complete and Email back to you for Orders, Information, Enquires at the Click of a Button (I will cover this in a separate chapter).

BTW these Tools are Great for Creating Graphics for T-shirts, Caps etc. Example at www.zazzle.co.nz/leftfieldnz

These Tools will also Future Proof Your Business as all the Tools can be Used across Media, whether it be Print, TV, or Online (The Internet) and on Mobile Devices like Cell Phones and Ipad.

Far to many SME Businesses do not take advantage of the Amazing Range of Free Tools out there to Create far better Flyers, Posters, Brochures and Menus etc. With these Free Tools you can make Professional Looking Material In-House and as Often as you Wish!

We have used this Suite of Tools to Create Books and Publicity Material for our Own Business at Creative Kiwis.

The Ultimate Desktop Publishing Book and CD by Bill Rosoman Dip CS

Together the Book and CD give You all the Tools and Knowledge you need to Get Creating.

For more Information and the Access to the Information and Tools You Need, See;

www.lulu.com/leftfieldnz or www.creativekiwis.com/dtpbook.html

# Desktop Publishing Software.

We have;

Scribus — Desktop Publishing
Gimp — Graphics, Pictures
Inkscape — Vector Graphics
Open Office — Wordprocessor etc.
Calibre — E-Book Reader and Converter
Ghostscript — Postscript Stuff
LittleCMS — Colour Management System

Cross platform (Windows, Linux, Mac)
All this software is free and legal

# Some Helpful Websites

www.lulu.com
www.lulu.com/leftfieldnz
www.scribus.net
www.gimp.org
www.Inkscape.org
www.openoffice.org
www.kubuntu.org
www.creativekiwis.com
http://wiki.scribus.net/index.php/Category:HOWTO
www.scribustutorials.net
www.desktoppublishingnews.net/
www.inkscapetutorials.net
www.thegimptutorials.net
www.desktop-publishing-software-review.com
http://desktoppub.about.com
www.blurb.com

While you can spend as much money as you like I guess buying Software, it does not necessarily mean it is any better than doing a great job using Free and Open Source Software.

This Suite of Programs generally have excellent Online Howtos and Tutorials as well as Access to many Fine Templates.

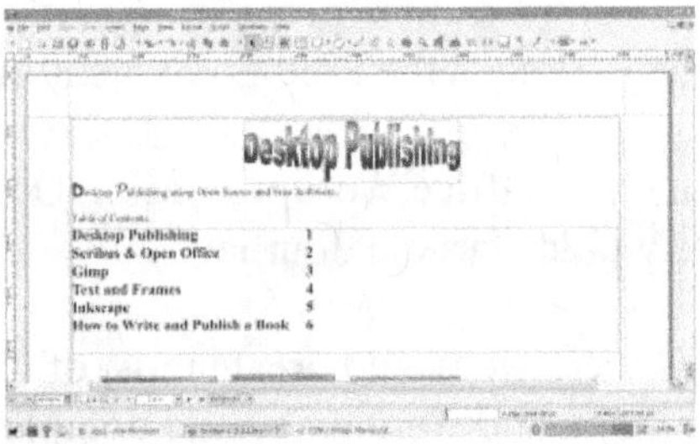


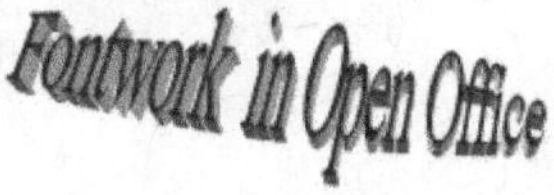


Scribus

http://www.scribustutorials.net/html/tutorials.html

Scribus I would describe as the end of the journey of creating your Desktop Publishing Masterpiece.

The last Program you use to pull together all your resources of Text, Pictures, Graphics Etc.

Scribus is a Desktop Publishing Application (DTP). With Scribus you can create all kinds of material ready for print or (if you prefer digital distribution) you can produce nicely formatted PDF. You can use Scribus, for example, for creating and publishing a magazine, books, posters, flyers, calendar, menu, brochure, or business cards. If you have used a DTP application before you will become familiar with Scribus quite quickly - it might not do everything the same way as other DTP software but the concepts are the same.

NB Scribus is not a Wordprocessor
NB Scribus does not save images normally

Scribus Shapes

Business Card

Brochure

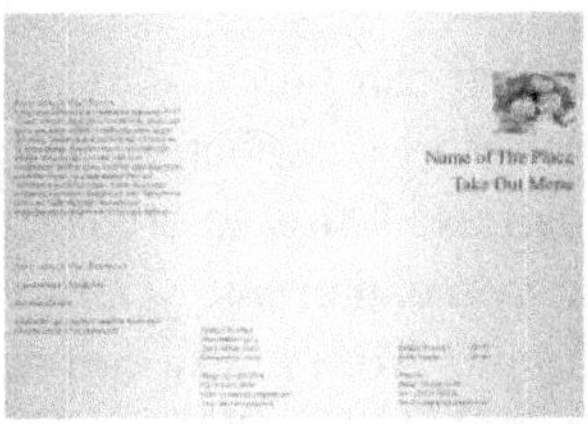


Menu

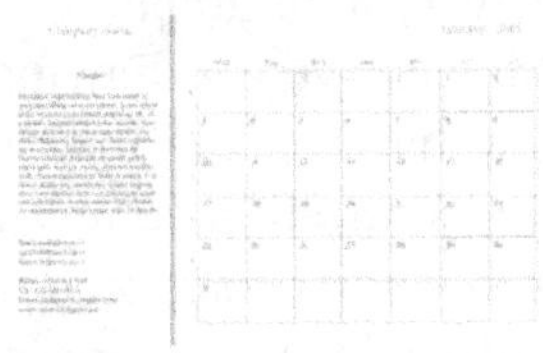

Calendar

Open Office

Open office is the Free Equivalent of Microsoft Office.

An Open Office Wordprocessing Document is were we would start our Journey.

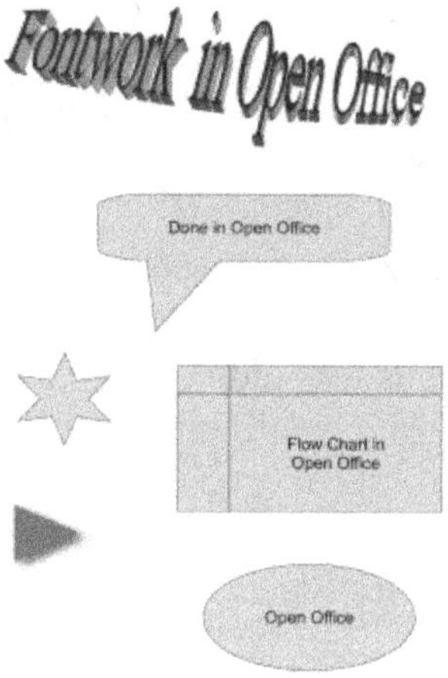


It is were we would create most of the text for our Creation and were we would complete things like spell check, auto-correction etc.

Open Office however also can do some very good Graphics and Fancy Text (FontWork). This best done in Open Office Drawing.

Your Open Office Word Document should be Saved As a Unformatted Text File. masterpiece.txt

An Open Office Drawing Can be Saved as that or Exported as a Graphic.

I have shown a few examples of what Open Office can do in the Howto.

http://www.tutorialsforopenoffice.org/
http://documentation.openoffice.org/tutorials/index.html
http://wiki.services.openoffice.org/wiki/Documentation/OOo3_User_Guides/Chapters

Writer (word processor)
Writer is a feature-rich tool for creating 1
etters, books, reports, newsletters, brochures, and other documents. You can insert graphics and objects from other components into Writer documents. Writer can export files to HTML, XHTML, XML, Adobe's Portable Document Format (PDF), and several versions of Microsoft Word files. It also connects to your email client.

Draw (vector graphics)
Draw is a vector drawing tool that can produce everything from simple diagrams or flowcharts to 3-D artwork. Its Smart Connectors feature allows you to define your own connection points. You can use Draw to create drawings for use in any of OOo's other components, and you can create your own clip art and add it to the Gallery. Draw can import graphics from many common formats and save them in over 20 formats, including PNG, HTML, PDF, and Flash.

Gimp

http://docs.gimp.org/2.6/en/

Gimp is mostly a Photo Manipulation Tool.

However it does many other things as well.

I have given a few examples.

Welcome to GIMP

GIMP is a multi-platform photo manipulation tool. GIMP is an acronym for GNU Image Manipulation Program. The GIMP is suitable for a variety of image manipulation tasks, including photo retouching, image composition, and image construction.

GIMP has many capabilities. It can be used as a simple paint program, an expert quality photo retouching program, an online batch processing system, a mass production image renderer, an image format converter, etc.

GIMP is expandable and extensible. It is designed to be augmented with plug-ins and extensions to do just about anything. The advanced scripting interface allows everything from the simplest task to the most complex image manipulation procedures to be easily scripted.

One of The GIMP's strengths is its free availability from many sources for many operating systems. Most GNU/Linuxdistributions include The GIMP as a standard application. The GIMP is also available for other operating systems such as Microsoft Windows™ or Apple's Mac OS X™ (Darwin). The GIMP is a Free Software application covered by the General Public License. The GPL provides users with the freedom to access and alter the source code that makes up computer programs.

GIMP Features and Capabilities

The following list is a short overview of some of the features and capabilities which GIMP offers you:

- A full suite of painting tools including brushes, a pencil, an airbrush, cloning, etc.
- Tile-based memory management, so image size is limited only by available disk space

- Sub-pixel sampling for all paint tools for high-quality anti-aliasing
- Full Alpha channel support for working with transparency
- Layers and channels
- A procedural database for calling internal GIMP functions from external programs, such as Script- Fu
- Advanced scripting capabilities
- Multiple undo/redo (limited only by disk space)
- Transformation tools including rotate, scale, shear and flip
- Support for a wide range of file formats, including GIF, JPEG, PNG, XPM, TIFF, TGA, MPEG, PS, PDF, PCX, BMP and many others
- Selection tools, including rectangle, ellipse, free, fuzzy, bezier and intelligent scissors
- Plug-ins that allow for the easy addition of new file formats and new effect filters.

Images

Images are the basic entities used by GIMP. Roughly speaking, an "image" corresponds to a single file, such as a TIFF or JPEG file. You can also think of an image as corresponding to a single display window, but this is not quite correct: it is possible to have multiple windows all displaying the same image. It is not possible to have a single window display more than one image, though, or for an image to have no window displaying it.

A GIMP image may be quite a complicated thing. Instead of thinking of it as something like a sheet of paper with a picture on it, think of it as more like a book, whose pages are called "layers". In addition to a stack of layers, a Gimp image may contain a selection mask, a set of channels, and a set of paths. In fact, GIMP provides a mechanism for attaching arbitrary pieces of data, called "parasites", to an image.

In GIMP, it is possible to have many images open at the same time. Although large images may use many megabytes of memory, GIMP uses a sophisticated tile-based memory management system that allows GIMP to handle very large images gracefully. There are limits, however, and having more memory available may improve system performance.

Layers

If an image is like a book, then a layer is like a page within the book. The simplest images contain only a single layer, and can be treated like single sheets of paper. Sophisticated GIMP users often deal with images containing many layers, even dozens of them. Layers need not be opaque, and they need not cover the entire extent of an image, so when you look at an image's display, you may see more than just the top layer: you may see elements of many layers.

Channels

In GIMP, Channels are the smallest units of subdivision in the stack of layers from which the image is constructed. Every Channel in a layer has exactly the same size as the layer to which it belongs, and, consequently consists of the same number of pixels. Every pixel can be regarded as a container which can be filled with a value ranging from 0 to 255.The exact meaning of this value depends on the type of channel, e.g. in the RGB colour model the value in the R-channel means the amount of red which is added to the colour of the different pixels, in the selection channel, the value denotes how strongly the pixels are selected, and in the alpha channel the values denote how transparent the corresponding pixels are.

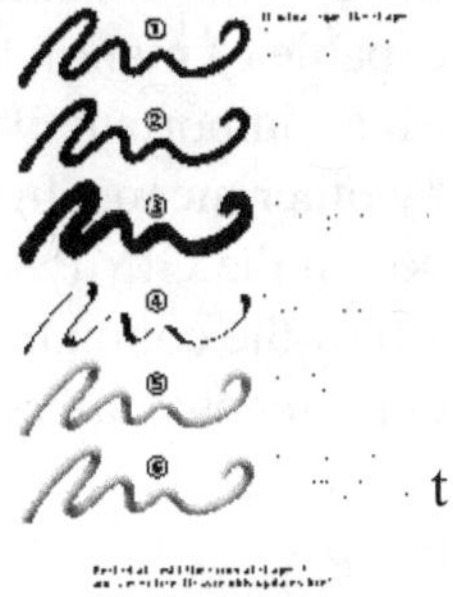

Selections

Often when modify an image, you only want a part of the image t
o be affected. The "selection" mechanism makes this possible.
Each image has its own selection, which you normally see as a moving dashed line separating the selected parts from the unselected parts (the so-called "marching ants" ). Actually this is a bit misleading: selection in GIMP is graded, not all-or-nothing, and really the selection is represented by a full-fledged grayscale channel. The dashed line that you normally see is simply a contour line at the 50%-selected level. At any time, though, you can visualize the selection channel in all its glorious detail by toggling the QuickMask button.

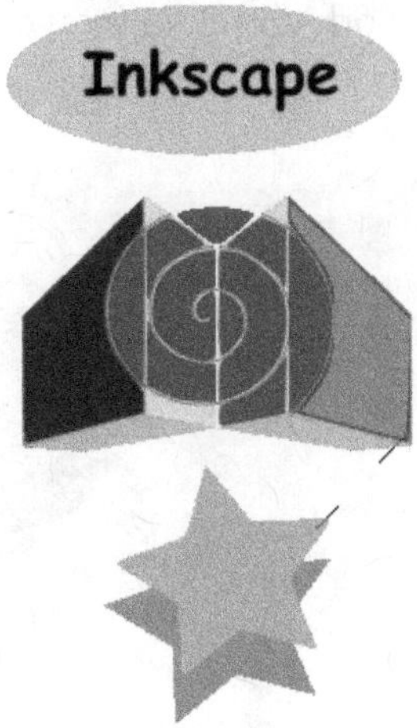

A large component of learning how to use GIMP effectively is acquiring the art of making good selections—selections that contain exactly what you need and nothing more. Because selection-handling is so centrally important, GIMP provides many tools for doing it: an assortment of selection-making tools, a menu of selection operations, and the ability to switch to Quick Mask mode, in which you can treat the selection channel as though it were a colour channel, thereby "painting the selection".

Undoing

When you make mistakes, you can undo them. Nearly everything you can do to an image is undoable. In fact, you can usually undo a substantial number of the most recent things you did, if you decide that they were misguided. GIMP makes this possible by keeping a history of your actions. This history consumes memory, though, so undoability is not infinite. Some actions use very little undo memory, so that you can do dozens of them before the earliest ones are deleted from this history; other types of actions require massive amounts of undo memory. You can configure the amount of memory GIMP allows for the undo history of each image, but in any situation, you should always be able to undo at least your 2-3 most recent actions. (The most important action that is not undoable is closing an image. For this reason, GIMP asks you to confirm that you really want to close the image if you have made any changes to it.)

Plug-ins

Many, probably most, of the things that you do to an image in GIMP are done by the GIMP application itself. However, GIMP also makes extensive use of "plug-ins", which are external programs that interact very closely with GIMP, and are capable of manipulating images and other GIMP objects in very sophisticated ways. Many important plug-ins are bundled with GIMP, but there are also many available by other means. In fact, writing plug-ins (and scripts) is the easiest way for people not on the GIMP development team to add new capabilities to GIMP.
All of the commands in the Filters menu, and a substantial number of commands in other menus, are actually implemented as plug-ins.

Scripts

In addition to plug-ins, which are programs written in the C language, GIMP can also make use of scripts. The largest number of existing scripts are written in a language called Script-Fu, which is unique to GIMP (for those who care, it is a dialect of the Lisp-like language called Scheme). It is also possible to write GIMP scripts in Python or Perl. These languages are more flexible and powerful than Script-Fu; their disadvantage is that they depend on software that does not automatically come packaged with GIMP, so they are not guaranteed to work correctly in every GIMP installation.

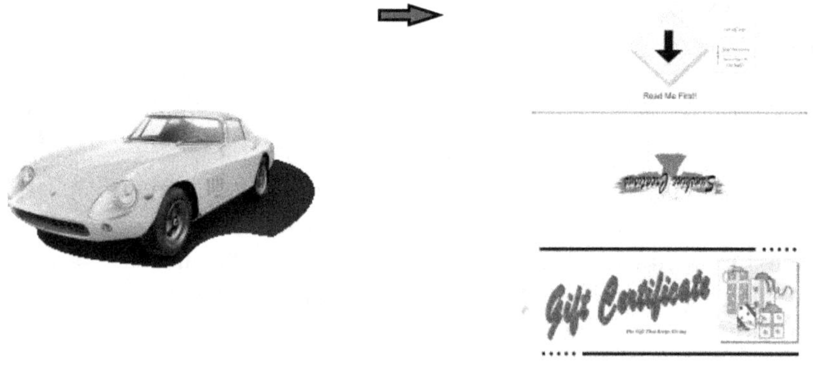


Inkscape

http://tavmjong.free.fr/INKSCAPE/MANUAL/html/index.php
http://www.libregraphicsworld.org/articles.php?article_id=12

Inkscape is a relatively young yet fast evolving generic vector graphics editor in the lines of Adobe Illustrator and Corel DRAW. The application can be run on Linux, Windows and Mac and it's freely distributable along with source code. Its main file format is SVG (Scalable Vector Graphics, a W3C standard recommended for publishing vector graphics on the Web)

What's unique in Inkscape? Did it really make sense creating yet another vector graphics tool?

There are not so many vector graphics editors, and most serious tools are part of the market for 10 to 20+ years. But this means that their developers are doomed to keep layers of legacy solutions and build new functionality on top of them. If you have a look at e.g. ACD Canvas which has duplicated tools, 3 tiers of toolbox, or at Adobe Illustrator, where e.g. editing, adding and removing nodes are three different tools. you'll see what we mean.

In Linux /usr/share/inkscape has a lot of templates and tutorials.

Summary
A Great Suite of Programs. The use of them can bring together a Great Project of Your Imagination.

We Start with Open Office Writer to Complete most of the Text for Our Masterpiece.

Next we find or create Photos and Graphics and Perhaps Fancy Fonts in Gimp, Inkscape and maybe Open Office Drawing.

Pulling it all together in Scribus.

Scribus Then Saves as a PDF or a good Print Post Script File for Printing and or as an Book, Brochure, E-Book for Distribution.

BTW
http://www.zamzar.com/ Is an Online Converter

I converted a MS Publisher File to Post Script Then Imported to Scribus.

Many thanks for the Online Information.

Bill Rosoman
www.webng.com/leftfieldnz
nugrownz@yahoo.com.au

## Some of the other Things You can do Besides Text in Scribus

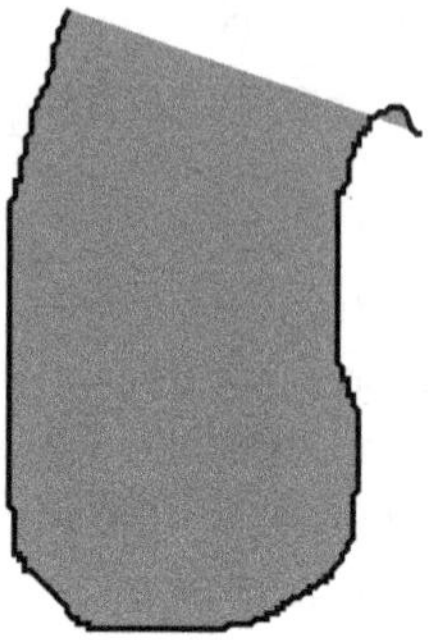

Creative Kiwis

www.creativekiwis.com

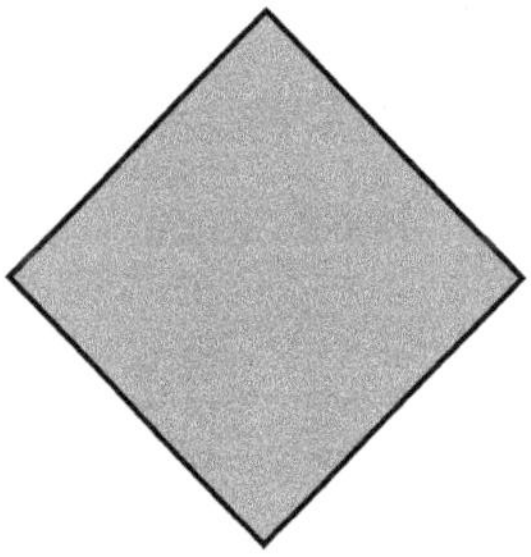

0 1 2 3 4 5 6 7 8 9

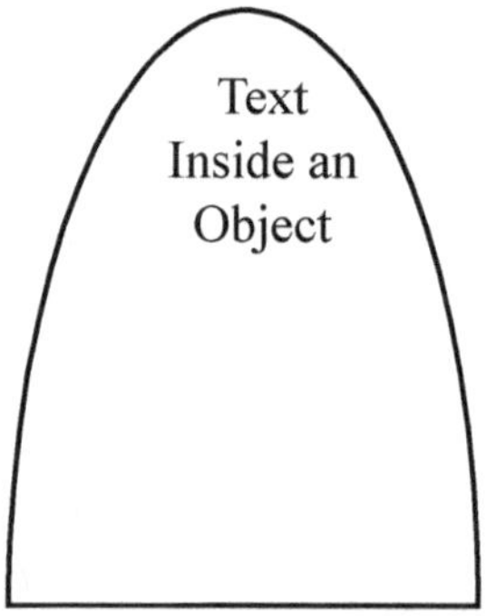


Table 1 Table 2 Table 3

Different Fonts Different Fonts

✤❄❄❄❄❒❄■

▼ ✦❑■▼▲

# Creating a Book Example.

The Plan

To Write a Book “The Ultimate Desktop Publishing Book”.

We need to create the manuscript document in Open Office Word Processor or Microsoft Office Word or another suitable program.

We need to save the Document as a TXT Text file for later use in Scribus. Goto File > Save As > Select Location, File Name and TXT Text Format. Then Save.

If you Re-Import to Office Use;
Unicode (UTF-8)
Times New Roman
English Dictionary
Paragraph Break LF (Line Feed)

In Office we can Spell Check, Auto-Correct etc. Do Not worry about the Document Layout Yet.

Prepare Manuscript
My suggestion is that you prepare the manuscript in Open Office Word Processor or Microsoft Office Word, TXT Text format.

I personally create different versions so if things go really wrong I have a backup of a previous version. I create a unique folder under /documents, say /books/ and then use File, Save As, and call it book1, book2 etc. I also do backups to another computer and/or to a usb pendrive and a Data CD.

The first rule of computing is to do backups. The second rule is to save your work and save often. You break these rules at your peril!

I carry the pendrive backup in a shoulder bag everywhere I go.

We need to consider what we are trying to achieve so we can plan and organise our document accordingly.

A lot of people will want to write a Novel or their Memoirs.

We have to also consider that we are doing a Book, maybe on a CD as a PDF file, Online as a PDF file, an EBook and perhaps as an Audio Book.

The general layout of the book is very important. It must look good and inviting. Not too much in capital letters, that is considered being rude. Nice spacing and paragraph breaks and an Index.

I Spell Check, Edit and Proof Read document
As you go along you need to keep an eye on the layout and do a spell check now and then.

One fundamental question you have to ask, if your manuscript is in English for instance, is which version of English will you use.

I guess if your target market is the USA then US English, if the target is Europe the UK English and of cause you could use NZ, SA, AUS or even International English.

Proof reading can be tricky as you become blinded by your own work, it is great then if you can get someone else to proof read the document.

Or you do it yourself and put up with the results I guess.

The best thing is to get into good housekeeping habits with your writing and with the using of the computer.

Regular backups are very important.

Regular spell checks and going back and checking the layout etc.

Of cause you should have the latest virus checker etc. on your computer and that it is up to date and fully operational. (Not a problem for me as I do not use windows but Linux were we do not get viruses and spyware).

Do not forget to save and back up your documents often!

Conclusion
So hopefully you have the the Spell Checking, Editing and Proof Reading under Control!

Next we need to create some graphics for the book front page etc. using The Gimp and Inkscape.

## The Gimp Picture/Graphic Manipulation/Edit

The Gimp is great for doing Pictures and Graphics.

To Scan a Picture. Make sure your Scanner is connected to the power and the computer and is turned on. Put the Picture into the Scanner. Open Gimp.
Use File > Create > xscanimage > Select your Scanner > Scan the Picture > If you Previewed, Select the Area you wish to scan by pulling down on the handlebars and Scan.

If you have scanned say two pictures at a time you need to cut and paste them.

To Cut and Paste > Select the Rectangle Select Tool (Top left) or Tools > Selection Tools > Rectangle Select. Highlight the area you wish to select using the mouse and click the Left Mouse Button and roll across the picture. Select Edit > Copy and then Edit > Paste as New Image.

Select File Save as, select a folder to save to, give the picture a name like pic1.jpg (make sure you add .jpg on the end). Select Save > Export > Save.

To Rotate an Image. If the image needs Rotating select > Image Transform and Rotate 90 or 180 degrees. Or use Tools > Transform Tools > Rotate.

To Resize an Image. You will see the size of the image at the top of the toolbar. To resize select > Image > Scale Image > for the Width Select say 900 pixels > Press TAB > Select Scale. If that is OK Select File Save. (This Size would be suitable to email or upload to a website).

You can also add text etc.

You can also use OCR, Optical Character Recognition (Copy Text).

To Crop a Pic
Of course if you crop the pic just to include the actually bits you want and this will reduce it further.

Use Gimp, and the "Select rectangular Regions" Tool, if the Toolbox is not visible go to Tools > Toolbox.

Select the part of a Pic you want > Press CTRL+C to Copy > Press Edit > Paste as New >

We can sharpen the pic, change the brightness and contrast and crop easily.

With Gimp I Took a Screen Shot of Each Programs About Screen.
Open > Help About
The Easy Option is to Press Print Screen > Button on Top Right of Keyboard (PrtSC).
If That does not work.
Use The Gimp
Open Gimp > File > Create > Screenshot
Select > Take a Screenshot of a Single Window > Tick Include Window Decoration.
Select the About Screen.
If you have to tidy the image up Select the Rectangle Select Tool > Place a Rectangle round the About Screen > Select Edit Copy > Select Edit > Paste As > New Image

Select > File > Save As > Name File file.gif > Select a Location for the File > Click Save > Export > Save
Do the Same for the Other Programs About Screens.

Have Fun!!!!!!!!!!!!!!!!!!!!!!!!!!!!!!!

You can adjust Brightness, whether Colour or Black and White Etc. Before Scanning.

To Cut out a part of the Scan
Tools > Selection Tools > Rect Set
Locate Corner you wish to cut out, hold down left mouse and move mouse to other point to cut
Select
Edit Copy > Edit paste as New >save Image (as below)

Save Image
File > Save As > Filename.jpg > Select Folder (Browse for Other Folders) > Save > Export (if asked) > OK
Or Save as filename.gif if you want background that is Transparent.

Scale Image
Image > Scale Image > Enter New Width > Press TAB

Image will scale to new size.
Save as above.

Using Images
It is better to open Open Office Draw and import the picture
Insert > Picture > From File > Locate Folder and File and Import.
Right click on picture and change Wrap to Optimal Wrap
Use Corner handles to resize image
Hold Left Mouse Button down to relocate Image.
File Print to Print Out

Rotate Image
Tools > Transform Tools > Rotate
Enter Angle + or – and Rotate

Pictures in Picasa
Use Picasa to view and organise your pictures. Picasa d
oes some wonderful things.

Run Picasa and wait for it to catalogue all the pictures on your hard drive. (Slow the first time you do it).

## Using Inkscape

I used Inkscape to do the Center Logo in Inkscape, it does a great job.

I Opened Inkscape and a New Document Appeared.
I Used File > Document Properties > Make it 1000 x 1000 pixels > Exit
Select From the Side Toolbar > Create Squares and Rectangles > Create a Square in the Centre.
You can Now Select a Colour from the Palette on The Bottom Toolbar.
I then Imported the About Graphics I had Previously done in The Gimp.
Grab the Handles to Resize and Move the Objects Into Place.
Use Object > Rotate 90 CW to Rotate each graphic so it fits in place correctly.
I Placed a Text Frame (On Left Toolbar) and the Typed in the Text.
I Used > Text > Text and Font (ON Top Toolbar) To Change the Font and Size and Orientation Etc.

I found that Inkscape will not Export as a gif file I Simply went
Edit > Select All > Edit > Copy
Then I went to The Gimp and went Edit > Paste > Paste as New Image
I then saved it as file.gif

So how is the task going?

My last book took many years, but seriously took nine months of work. I work nights so I was being paid to write my book between coping with customers.

Now you need to get on and finish the manuscript!

Best of luck and we will see you soon.

## Obtain an ISBN number

Now your book is taking shape we need to sharpen our pencil and get organised so we can get the book published and up and out there!

So the first thing we have to do is get an ISBN number.

An ISBN number is the Books unique International number. You can not publish a book without one effectively!

In New Zealand ISBN numbers are controlled by the NZ National Library and can be obtained from

http://www.natlib.govt.nz/services/get-advice/publishing/isbn/isbn-application

Email ISBN@natlib.govt.nz

Overseas there is places like
www.isbn.org

It is a matter of filling in an online form of the Book title, author etc. and within a small amount of time you have an ISBN number.

I create a text file with information about the book;

ISBN Book Catalogue

Main Title: The Ultimate Desktop Publishing Book
Personal Author: Rosoman Bill; 1948 -
Imprint: Hamilton New Zealand: Self, 2010
Collation: 54p: 18.90cm 24.58cm
Abstract: The Ultimate Desktop Publishing Book
Desktop Publishing using Free Open Source Software. A Brilliant Book giving You All the Tools and Examples You Need to Create That Masterpiece within You.

Creating and publishing a magazine, books, posters, flyers, calendar, menu, award certificates, or business cards could Never Be Easier.

Language: English
ISBN: 978-0-473-17409-5
Subject: DTP, Desktop Publishing. Free Software, Free Open Source Software, FOSS,

Format: Book, EBook

keywords
DTP, Desktop Publishing. Free Software, Free Open Source Software, FOSS, Scribus, Gimp, Inkscape, Calibre, Software, Books, Flyers, Brochures, Menu, Posters

publisher's address and contact details
Bill Rosoman
PO Box 4155
Hamilton East 3247

contact person, telephone number and address if different from the publisher's address
Bill Rosoman

Telephone 021-233-5427
Email leftfieldnz@gmail.com

date of publication
2010

It should also be remembered that you have to send two copies of your Book to the Legal Deposit Office, well at least in New Zealand that is what you have to do.

## Create a Book Cover

When you upload the book to www.lulu.com you can just select the Front Cover they provide or you can create your own. or get it Published elsewhere you will still probably need a Front Cover.

To create your own you can use Gimp Image Creator/Manipulator or similar and Inkscape Vector Graphics.

Open Open Office Draw or The Gimp.

In Open Office Draw.
I Created the Fancy Title Using Fontwork on the Bottom Toolbar.
I Put in a Text Frame and Added the Text
I Copied the Logo I Created by Copying in The Gimp and Then Pasting in Office Draw.

Now you can add Text and maybe a Graphic or Picture. I have been doing the initial work in Open Office Draw, then exporting as a jpg graphic and resizing and finishing in The Gimp.

Next Resize the Image in the Gimp. Use Image > Resize and make the size 648.41 x 978.96mm 25.528" x 38.542" 1838 x 2775 pixels for a novel size book or This Book Cover 801.16 x 1051.28 mm 31.542" x 41.389" or 2271 x 2980 pixels. You will need to unlink the Image Size, Width and Height Link.

You need to have this graphic available and the correct size when you upload the book.

## Scribus

Scribus is the Tool we use to Pull Our Masterpiece Together.

Open Scribus and Choose the type of Document you wish. In order to make measurements easier to understand set the Default Unit to Millimetres under options on the right of the New Document Dialog Box.

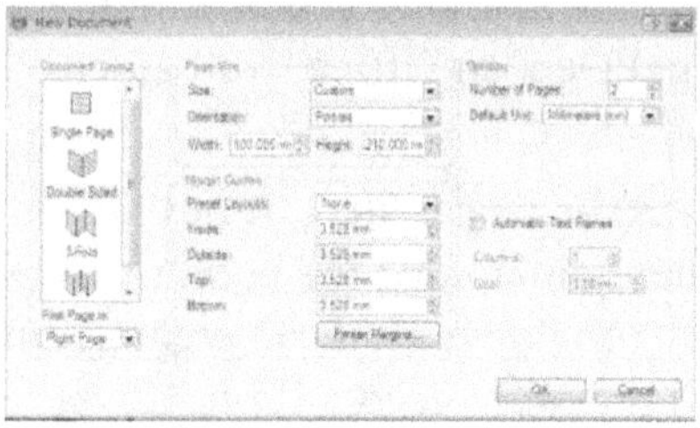

Also set the Number of Pages. Once you have done this click OK. You will see that Scribus Opens with both Pages displayed as in the Image below.

You must prepare your Images and Graphics first and Place Them in a Folder specifically created for this Job.

Open Scribus
Click New Document > One Page > Make the Size > Custom >
A Novel is usually 6" x 9" or 152.4mm x 228.6mm.
Crown Quarto 189.0mm x 245.80mm 7.44" x 9.68" is for things like manuals and handbooks and this Book.
Tick Text Frame > OK

Now Click Page > Copy > OK
Goto Page 2
Click on the Text Frame and Bring it Down the Page a Bit. Enough to Put in a New Text Frame for the Page Number.

Click on the Page Frame and Create a Small Text Frame at the Top of the Page.

Click on the Edit the Text, Story Editor on the Top Toolbar.
Click Insert > Character > Page Number and then do the Same Again.
Click the Green Tick on the Left of the Toolbar.
You Should see the Page Number in the Text Frame.
If Necessary Center the Frame.

Now with Your View as Page 2
Select Page > Copy > Copy Page 2 > Number of Copies > 70 (An Even Number) > At End > OK
You Now Have a 72 Page Document.

Now Select File > Save > Give the File a Name and Select a Location > Save

I have created many text files for the various chapters and text that I want to Insert Into Scribus.

Select the First Page Text Frame > Click on the Edit the Text, Story Editor on the Top Toolbar.
Select Load From File > Locate Your Text Files and Select One.
The First Time you Need to Create some Font Styles.
Select Edit > Styles > New > Name it Text > Select Font Times New Roman Regular > Select 10pt Size > Select Align Left > OK
Create Another for Centering > Select Font Times New Roman Regular > Select 10pt Size > Select Align Center > OK
Create Another for the Header > Select Font Times New Roman Bold > Select 14pt Size > Select Align Left > OK

Next I Press CTRL+A and Select Text From the Pulldown Menu on the Top Toolbar.

I use some Bullets as well.
Put the Cursor in Front of the Text you wish to Bullet and Select > Insert > Character > Bullet
Repeat this for Each Line You wish to have a Bullet, Or Copy and Paste the Bullet.

For a Heading Highlight the Text and Select Heading from The Style Menu.

The Body should only use New Times Roman font at 10.0 point. Maybe up to New Times Roman font 16 point for headings.

A trick is that the correct font must also include all the empty spaces as well.

Of cause a lot of Layout is subjective and is subject to your personal choice.

You also need to be consistent, with layout, font, size, etc.

Scribus Desktop Publishing
.sla

Open Office Document
.odt

Microsoft Office Document
.doc

Rich Text Format Document
.rtf

Text File
.txt

A Novel is usually 6" x 9" or 152.4mm x 228.6mm.

Crown Quarto 189.1mm x 245.89mm 7.444" x 9.681" is for things like manuals and handbooks and this Book.

More information is available at sites like
www.lulu.com

Now you Can Click the Green Tick to Exit the Text Editor and Return to Scribus.

You Can now add Graphics.
Grab the Insert Image Frame from the Top Toolbar > Create a Frame on the Page > Right Click on the Frame > Click Get Image > Locate Image and Click on It.
Now Right Click Image again > Select Properties > Select Shape > Text Flows Around Shape > Rounding
Select > Image > Scale to Frame Size Proportional
Adjust the Frame Size and Location
Right Click > Select Level > Raise to Top

Go though the Document Putting Graphics and Adjusting the Layout.

Creating a Table of Contents requires some configuration in your Document settings before it will be able to generate the list for you.
Go to File > Document Setup and then to the Document Item Attributes screen. These attributes are metadata that can be attached to any item for any number of reasons. For example, you may wish to put some author's details in a frame's attributes list. For now, all we need to do is create a new Document Attribute by clicking on the Add button. Just put TOC in the name field and leave the rest blank/default.

Creating a TOC

There are three more steps to actually use the TOC generator.
Create or Select an existing empty frame in your document that will hold the table of contents. Right Click on the Text Frame and Note the Name of the Frame > Maybe text85

Go to File->Document Setup and then to the Table of Contents and Indexes screen. Add a new Table of Contents, if necessary, and select TOC as its item attribute name.

Go through the Document Right click on those text frames that should generate an entry in the table of contents. Click on Attributes... (or go to Item >Attributes). If no attribute with the name TOC exists, add one by selecting it from the list. You also have to put in a Value, this should be the title of the entry in the table of contents. Click OK

Refresh the Table of Contents by Going to the TOC Text Frame and Selecting it

Then selecting Extras > Generate Table Of Contents.

Tables are not handled so elegantly. If you insert a blank table, Scribus simply groups individual text boxes together as cells. You must ungroup them to add text to them. As a result, tables do not import well. One solution is to create tables in another program (such as OpenOffice.org Writer) and save that file as a PDF, which Scribus can import as a graphic.

Colour Calibration
Using the free tools at the site of LittleCMS, you can calibrate your monitor under GnuLinux, much like you would do with the Adobe Gamma utility under Mac or Windows.

The most important aspect of using a colour management system is remembering to activate it! When it comes to exporting our final PDFs, we'll go over this in detail, but for now have a look at File > Export > Save Page as PDF. In the dialog box that appears, choose the color tab. If you have LittleCMS installed, you will see a drop-down menu under PDF/X-3 if possible. This menu contains the press pro-files – consult your printer and choose the relevant one.

[Match Colors That Print] Finally, if you wish to design publications, you need to ensure colors you see on screen match colors that print. For this, you need to install a special and separate piece of software, called a Color Management System, or CMS. Windows and Macintosh come with a CMS built-in, called ICM and ColorSync, respectively. Under GnuLinux, you need to install a free CMS, called LittleCMS. Download and follow the instructions at littlecms.com. You can also install versions of this under Windows and Macintosh. For this tutorial, LittleCMS is not necessary, though quite helpful.

Special Output of File
Now Imagine that you work in an Office as part of a Team and you want to send this Page to another colleague to add his or her contribution. They also have Scribus installed on their computer. You need to make sure that you send them all the necessary files.

Firstly you will need to create a folder to place the files in. I created a folder in C:/scribus called output.
Next Click on File > Collect for Output from the main menu

A dialog will appear asking you to choose a directory. Choose the directory you have just created and then click the OK button.

Below you can see the folder with the files in it that Scribus has copied. You can burn these files to a disk or copy them onto a memory stick. All your original files are still on your Hard Drive in your Jobs Folder. This method ensures that all the correct files are packaged and also you don't run the risk of accidentally deleting or moving the Original Files.

Create PDF File
Now you have completed the document you need to convert it to a PDF file or PS File to be able to have the Completed Document Print Ready.

I have found a PDF gives you the easiest and best results when uploading your Book for Publishing and Printing.

In Scribus
Click Saves as PDF on the Top Toolbar > Unless the Errors are Real Serious and Need Correcting Select Compatibility > PDF/X3 if Possible
Select Compress Text and Vector Graphics
Select Fonts TAB > Select Embed All
At the Top You can Change the Path and File Name > Select Save
Now you have a PDF file Ready to go.

Save the PDF file then open it and check the result for page breaks and layout etc.

If you have trouble making a PDF file especially if it complains about embedding fonts, go back to your document and make sure you only have the New Times Roman font. Then try again. This is the only problem I had in making a PDF file in the past, though Scribus seems to overcome this limitation.

When your finally document is ready, check it for the layout and go back and make any corrections needed.

The Other Option is a EPS (Post Script File)
Select File > Export > EPS > Change the Path and File Name if Desired > Press Save

I think you are much better if you would like to print the masterpiece yourself to use the PDF or EPS file as it s eems that Scribus does not do a good job of Printing!

## Other Information

Automatic Text Frames
Scribus puts all the content inside 'Text Frames'. You can create these manually or ask Scribus to automatically place the frames on each page at the same internal height and width of the margin settings. If you wish to automate this then select 'Automatic Text Frames'.

You can then choose how many columns of text you wish to appear within the text frame and the gap between each column.

Everything is framed

All elements of a document are arranged in frames, which you can arbitrary position on the page. These are represented on the screen with a dotted edge; which is red for a selected element. Each frame has a tab (or a small square) on all four corners, which can be held and dragged with the mouse to change the size of the frame.

One way of making the exact positioning of elements easier is to make the help lines magnetic with the View/Snap to Guides command – this means that the edges of the element will automatically “snap” onto the help lines. The space of these guides can be changed in the program options, reached by means of the Edit/Preferences... menu command. Behind the Guides tab, you will find the necessary options. You can create a rough grid with Major Grid Spacing, and then a fine grid with Minor Grid Spacing.

Furthermore, you can also specify whether the help lines are to be shown in front of or behind the elements.

Text

So how does the text get into the frames? There are two possibilities: The first is to click on the Edit Contents of Frame icon and enter the text in the desired frames. That is somewhat laborious with longer texts. It is therefore advisable to enter the text into a text editor or word processor first and then to load this into the frame. To do this, select the appropriate text

File > Document Setup

Great Now you can Send it to a Printer or Upload Online.

# To Publish and Print Your Book on Lulu.com (On Demand Printing)

Publish Your Masterpiece on www.lulu.com a Publish On Demand Website (POD).

www.blurb.com is a similar site.

As mentioned in a previously, you need and ISBN number, your finished document as a PDF file, a front page graphic and a lulu account.

Go to www.lulu.com and upload and publish your book and you are away!

You need to Create an Account On to Lulu.com
You need to Log On to Lulu.com
Goto My Lulu
New Project
Upload pdf document and front cover
Set your prices
Make available to the public
And then wait for the sales

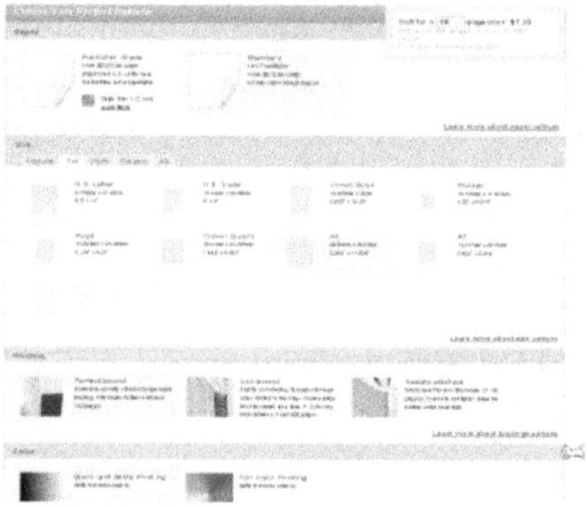

Promote on Google Books, Youtube etc.
Places like Google Books is a great place to spread the word about your new wonderful creation.

On Google Books you need a summary of the book, a sample PDF file and a front page graphic.

Sign up for Google Books and then Log on to Google Books.

Follow the instructions to upload and enter your book on their website.

http://books.google.com/

Youtube is a good place to put a promo about your book. I created a simple slide show, added an audio, created a movie and uploaded to Youtube.

www.youtube.com/

I have made a small slideshow promoting my books and put it onto
http://www.youtube.com/watch?v=0Lze_Vl_g0A

These sites may be able to promote your books.

www.stumbleupon.com

http://del.icio.us/
www.facebook.com
www.bebo.com
www.trademe.co.nz
www.ebay.com

Order Some Copies of Your Book from Lulu
To Order an Authors copy of a Book from Lulu
log on to www.lulu.com
Go to My Lulu
Click on Title Buy Icon on right of title
Add to Cart
Enter Quantity
Update Cart
Checkout
Pay by Credit Card or Paypal.

## Some Interesting Websites

www.creativekiwis.com
www.gimp.org
www.openoffice.org
www.mozilla.com/firefox
www.printondemand.com/
http://en.wikipedia.org/wiki/Print_on_demand
www.blurb.com/
www.iuniverse.com
www.unlimitedpublishing.com/
www.writersworld.co.uk/
www.writershelper.com/self-published-author.html
www.spacejock.com.au/SelfPublishing.html
http://66.89.113.16/doc2pdf/
www.pdfforge.org/products/pdfcreator
www.pdf995.com
www.webng.com/writernz
www.lulu.com/leftfieldnz
http://books.google.com/
www.youtube.com/
http://books.google.com
www.sfwa.org/beware/printondemand.html
www.authorhouse.com/GetPublished/Products_Promotion.asp
www.natlib.govt.nz/services/get-advice/publishing/isbn
www.webng.com/leftfieldnz/getalife.html
www.natlib.govt.nz/publishers
www.spacejock.com.au/PrintOnDemand.html
www.equilibriumbooks.com/faqs.htm
www.self-publishers.org.nz/index.htm

www.authors.org.nz/info_for_writers/faq.htm
media-convert.com/
www.zamzar.com/
www.pixlr.com/
http://docs.google.com/
www.zoho.com

I have had some sales on Lulu

## Conclusion

Well hopefully you have now completed the task and it is now time to go fishing!

More information is available at sites like
www.lulu.com

Best of luck in your life and with your writing!

websites
www.webng.com/writernz
or
www.webng.com/leftfieldnz

TTFN

# Creating a Brochure Example.

The Plan

To Create a Brochure “The Ultimate Desktop Publishing Brochure”.

Creating The Ultimate Desktop Publishing
Brochure Example.

Prepare Manuscript

My suggestion is that you prepare the manuscript in Open Office Word Processor or Microsoft Office Word, TXT Text format.

Conclusion

Follow some of the Hints in the “Creating a Book Example”.

So hopefully you have the the Spell Checking, Editing and Proof Reading under Control!

Next we need to create some graphics, using Open Office Draw.

Office Draw

I Opened Open Office Draw.
I Made a Fontwork Text (On Bottom Toolbar)
Click on Fontwork, Pull The Text Frame Across the Page
Double Click on Fontwork and Add Your Text
I Adjusted the Size and Font Colour.
I then Saved > Clicked on the Fontwork Graphic > File > Export > Select a Location and Filename > Select File Type as GIF (Gives us a Transparent Image).

The Other Graphics I had from the Previous “Creating a Book Example”.

Scribus

Scribus is the Tool we use to Pull Our Masterpiece Together.

Open Scribus
Click New Document > One Page > Make the Size > A4 > Landscape
Tick Text Frame > OK

Now Select Page > Copy > Copy One Page > Number of Copies > At End,

I have created a text file for the Brochure that I want to Insert Into Scribus.

Select the First Page

You Can now add Graphics.

First the Header.
Grab the Insert Image Frame from the Top Toolbar > Create a Frame on the Top of the Page > Right Click on the Frame > Click Get Image > Locate Image and Click on It.
Now Right Click Image again > Select Properties > Select Shape > Text Flows Around Shape > Rounding
Select > Image > Scale to Frame Size Proportional or Non-Proportional. See Which is Best.
Adjust the Frame Size and Location
Right Click > Select Level > Raise to Top

Now do the Same for the Other Graphics.

Now Create a Page Text Frame > Click on the Edit the Text, Story Editor on the Top Toolbar.
Select Load From File > Locate Your Text Files and Select One.
The First Time you Need to Create some Font Styles.
Select Edit > Styles > New > Name it Text > Select Font Times New Roman Regular > Select 10pt Size > Select Align Left > OK
Create Another for Centering > Select Font Times New Roman Regular > Select 10pt Size > Select Align Center > OK
Create Another for the Header > Select Font Times New Roman Bold > Select 14pt Size > Select Align Left > OK

Next I Press CTRL+A and Select Text From the Pulldown Menu on the Top Toolbar.

Now you Can Click the Green Tick to Exit the Text Editor and Return to Scribus.

Go though the Document Putting Text and Graphics in and Adjusting the Layout.

Select Page Two and  Put Text and Graphics in and Adjusting the Layout

Conclusion

Follow some of the Hints in the “Creating a Book Example”.

When your finally document is ready, check it for the layout and go back and make any corrections needed.

# Creating an Award Certificate Example.

The Plan

To Create “An Award Certificate”.

Creating an Award CertificateExample.

Prepare Manuscript

My suggestion is that you prepare the manuscript in Open Office Word Processor or Microsoft Office Word, TXT Text format.

Conclusion

Follow some of the Hints in the “Creating a Book Example”.

So hopefully you have the the Spell Checking, Editing and Proof Reading under Control!

Next we need to create some graphics, using Open Office Draw.

Office Draw

I Opened Open Office Draw.
I Made a Fontwork Text (On Bottom Toolbar)
Click on Fontwork, Pull The Text Frame Across the Page
Double Click on Fontwork and Add Your Text
I Adjusted the Size and Font Colour.
I then Saved > Clicked on the Fontwork Graphic > File > Export > Select a Location and Filename > Select File Type as GIF (Gives us a Transparent Image).

I Used Google Images to Find a Suitable Template for my Award Certificate.

Scribus

Scribus is the Tool we use to Pull Our Masterpiece Together.

Open Scribus
Click New Document > One Page > Make the Size > A5 >
Tick Text Frame > OK

I have created a text file for the Award that I want to Insert Into Scribus.

You Can now add Graphics.

First the Border Template.

Grab the Insert Image Frame from the Top Toolbar > Create a Frame on the Page > Right Click on the Frame > Click Get Image > Locate Image and Click on It.
Now Right Click Image again > Select Properties > Select Image > Scale to Frame Size Proportional or Non-Proportional. See Which is Best.
Adjust the Frame Size and Location
Right Click > Select Level > Lower to Bottom

Next the Header.

Grab the Insert Image Frame from the Top Toolbar > Create a Frame on the Top of the Page > Right Click on the Frame > Click Get Image > Locate Image and Click on It.
Now Right Click Image again > Select Properties > Select Shape > Text Flows Around Shape > Rounding
Select > Image > Scale to Frame Size Proportional or Non-Proportional. See Which is Best.
Adjust the Frame Size and Location
Right Click > Select Level > Raise to Top

Now Create a Page Text Frame > Click on the Edit the Text, Story Editor on the Top Toolbar.
Select Load From File > Locate Your Text Files and Select One.
The First Time you Need to Create some Font Styles.
Select Edit > Styles > New > Name it Text > Select Font Times New Roman Regular > Select 10pt Size > Select Align Left > OK
Create Another for Centering > Select Font Times New Roman Regular > Select 10pt Size > Select Align Center > OK
Create Another for the Header > Select Font Times New Roman Bold > Select 14pt Size > Select Align Left > OK

Next I Press CTRL+A and Select Text From the Pulldown Menu on the Top Toolbar.

Now you Can Click the Green Tick to Exit the Text Editor and Return to Scribus.

Go though the Document Putting Graphics and Adjusting the Layout.

Conclusion

Follow some of the Hints in the "Creating a Book Example".

When your finally document is ready, check it for the layout and go back and make any corrections needed.

# The Ultimate Desktop Publishing CD.

We have a Special Priced Ultimate Desktop Publishing CD to Compliment the Book.
$15 + FREE Shipping and handling.

The CD Contains all the Software, Resources and Information You Need to Write and Publish a Book, Produce a Newspaper or Brochure.

All You Need is the Time and Inspiration!

All the tools and resources you need for creating and publishing a magazine, books, posters, flyers, calendar, menu, or business cards

The CD Contains;

| | |
|---|---|
| * All The Necessary Windows Software | |
| * Scribus | Desktop Publishing |
| * Gimp | Graphics, Pictures |
| * Inkscape | Vector Graphics |
| * Open Office | Wordprocessor etc. |
| * Ghostscript | Postscript Stuff |
| * PDF creator | |
| * LittleCMS | Colour Management System |
| * Calibre | E-Book Reader/Converter |

* Cross platform (Windows, Linux, Mac)
* All this software is free and legal

It also Includes some extra fonts.

* Some Sample Templates
* Some Howtos and Tutorials
* Some Free E-Books
* Access to Our How to Get Published Book
* Access to Our How to Get Published Course
* Access to Our How we can help You Get Published

The Special Price is $15 + FREE Shipping and Handling as a CD to Compliment the Book.

A Couple of Scribus Howtos are available at;

http://www.esnips.com/web/leftfieldnz-Scribus/

http://www.esnips.com/doc/b61cfeaf-9e31-4d47-9f1e-83d774349bc0/scribushowto

http://www.esnips.com/doc/a31ac46d-cf5a-435a-82d2-016a6411688a/noveltemplate

# The Ultimate Desktop Publishing Book

# Calibre E-Book Reader and Converter

Calibre is excellent Free Open Source Software which enables you to read E-Books in various formats, Convert to another format, download and read magazines and news papers and save to many devices like E-readers and Cell Phones.

Add an E-Book
Make or Download Your E-Books. I found heaps of free E-Books Online.

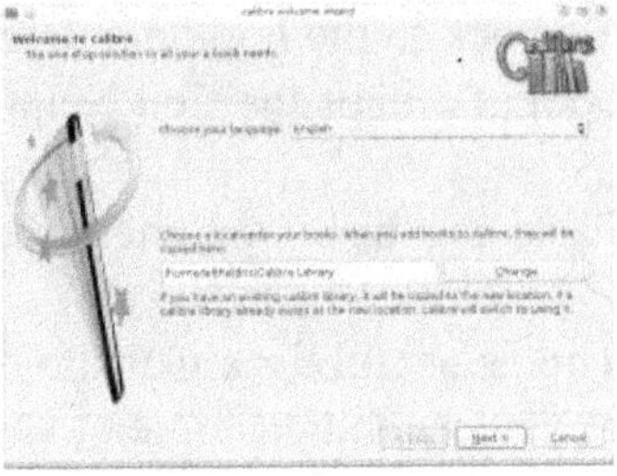

Click on Add Books
Locate the E-Books in a Folder.
Either highlight one E-Book or just Click OK to Add all the E-Books in that Folder.

Edit Meta Information
This allows you to Enter or Edit the Author, Book Title, Publisher Etc.

Convert E-Books
This allows you to Convert an E-Book from say PDF to EPUB for a Kindle or Sony Reader.

View
This is to View Your E-Books. With the EPUB Book You can make the Font Larger or Smaller.

Fetch News
This allows you to Download Newspapers and Magazines.

I Downloaded Wired Magazine, The Irish independent, The Guardian, Stuff.co.nz

Fabulous and all for Free.

Send to Device
This enables you to send to a Device like a Kindle or Cell Phone, or to a Pen-drive or Hard drive or SD Card Etc.

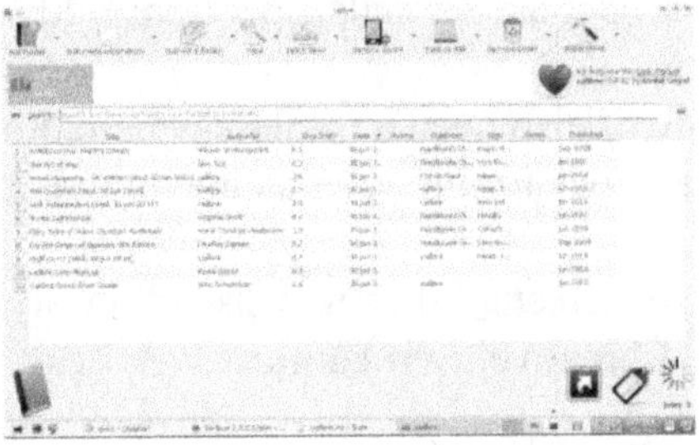

Save to Disk
Offers to save different formats like all Your EPUB E-Books to Disk in a Single Folder.

Remove Books
You can Remove your E-Books.

Preferences

## Create a Website

Now you have a wonderful Book or Project Completed you will need a website to promote it and sell some Books.

Create a Sample PDF Document
========================

Go back to the book document in Scribus and copy a section as a sample of your book. Perhaps the first chapter or two and including the Table of Contents.

Paste as a new Document then save as booksample then convert to a PDF file.

This is useful for a website or on sites like Google Books or for sending to potential reviewers and customers.

Create a website
============

It would be great to create a website to promote yourself and your books.

http://www.wikihow.com/Make-a-Website
http://www.wikihow.com/Create-a-Simple-Web-Page-With-HTML

There are plenty of free websites hosts if you do not wish to spend much money.

We currently use www.webng.com they have proved to be very good.

Our Business Site is at www.creativekiwis.com

I have of late created the basic webpage in Open Office and then save as an .html file. I have then edited the file in NVU or similar web editor.

http://www.net2.com/nvu/download.html

You need a front page which is normally index.html and then maybe a book page. NB do not use capitals, spaces or odd symbols in a webpage name.

You will also need a folder say called images for the various pictures, and a folder called docs for the various documents you will have.

I have also started using Cascading Style Sheets. Example at
www.creativekiwis.com/css.web1.css

CSS Make for a Uniform and Good looking Website, they also make it easy to change the Whole Website, simply by editing the Style Sheet.

I like to keep a website very simple and have only two or three clicks to a sale.

So your website will look like;
/docs
sample.pdf
/images
frontcover.jpg

In the Root/Main Folder
books.html
index.html
orders.html
enquire.html

If you have a look at our site at www.creativekiwis.com you will get the idea.

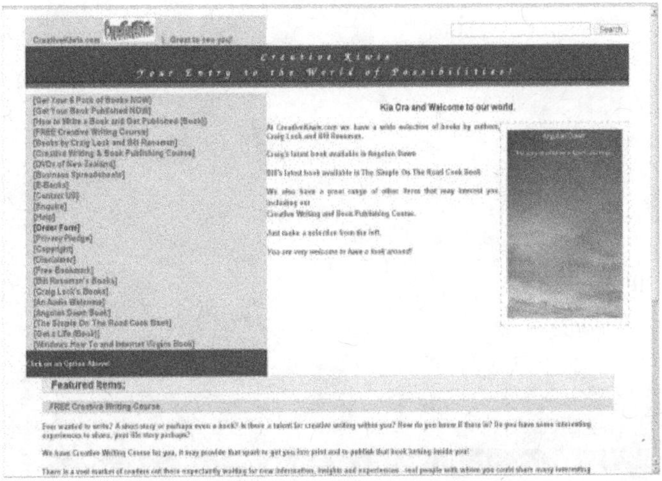


Right click on a page and go view source, this will show you the code we have used to create the website.

Logon to your website say www.webng.com and go to the file manager. Create the folders and then upload the webpages, images and documents. Then have a look and see if things have turned out as planned.

Offer the samplebook.pdf you created as a free download.

Another good idea is sell your books with a Paypal option. Check out www.paypal.com

We do not need a Shopping Cart as we use lulu or paypal and find them great and trusted by Our Customers.

Google Books is another place you can upload y
known you have a book available.

I have put up a Ezine page on Our Website as an
www.creativekiwis.com/ezines/index.html

Conclusion
=========

Phew! now we are getting there!

More information is available at sites like
www.lulu.com

Best of luck.

websites
=========

www.webng.com/writernz
or
www.webng.com/leftfieldnz

TTFN

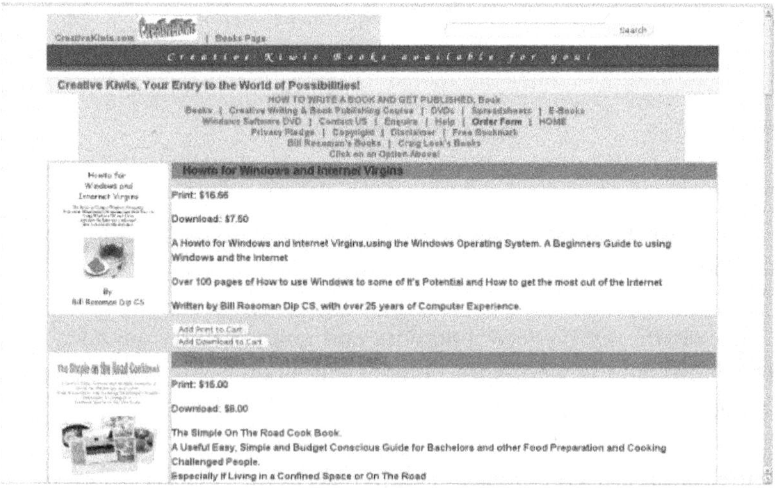

# Creating a Poster Example.

The Plan
=======

To Create a Poster “Wanted Dead or Alive” Poster.

Creating a Poster “Wanted Dead or Alive” Poster.

Prepare Manuscript
My suggestion is that you prepare the manuscript in Open Office Word Processor or Microsoft Office Word, TXT Text format.

Conclusion
=========

Follow some of the Hints in the “Creating a Book Example”.

So hopefully you have the the Spell Checking, Editing and Proof Reading under Control!

Next we need to create some graphics, using Open Office Draw and The Gimp.

Open Office Draw
==============

I Opened Open Office Draw.
I Made a Fontwork Text (On Bottom Toolbar)
Click on Fontwork, Pull The Text Frame Across the Page
Double Click on Fontwork and Add Your Text
I Adjusted the Size and Font Colour.
I then Saved > Clicked on the Fontwork Graphic > File > Export > Select a Location and Filename > Select File Type as GIF (Gives us a Transparent Image).

The Thank-You Graphic I made in The Gimp.

I Created a New Graphic 200x70 pixels
I Selected the Text Tool
Entered Than-You Text and then Selected the Font, Font Size and Center.
I then Selected, Filters > Alpha to Logo > 3D Outline.
I then Selected the Rectangle Tool Copied the Text and Pasted as a New Image.
I the Filled the Background and Saved.

Scribus
=====

Scribus is the Tool we use to Pull Our Masterpiece Together.

Open Scribus
Click New Document > One Page > Make the Size > A4 > Landscape
Tick Text Frame > OK

Now Select Page > Copy > Copy One Page > Number of Copies > At End,

I have created a text file for the Brochure that I want to Insert Into Scribus.

Select the First Page

You Can now add Graphics.

And there you have your Poster.

# PDF Smart Form Document

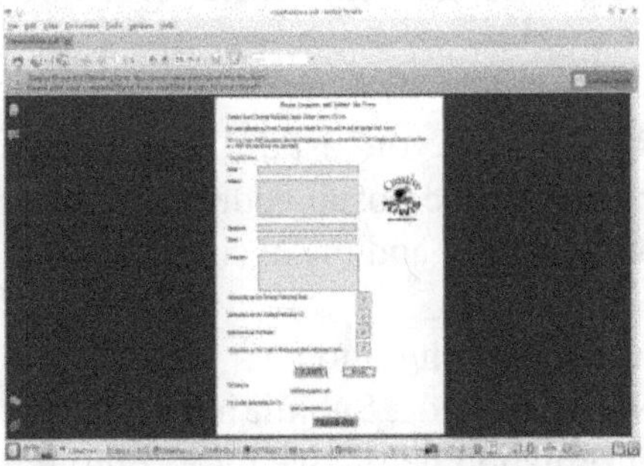

Create a smart PDF document with Scribus
Original Howto by Sukrit Dhandhania
http://www.linuxuser.co.uk/tutorials/create-a-smart-pdf-document-with-scribus/

Introduction
You can Create a PDF form, so People can Complete the Form and Print it or Email it back to you. Very Handy!

Add text boxes
We want a Header, Then the fields we are looking to capture are Name, Address, Phone Number, Email Address and Comments. Create text boxes to the left-hand side of the document, one on top of the other. You can also do some styling for these text boxes. Make sure they are smaller than the title text, but clearly legible.

Fonts and colours
Select all the text you added and right-click on it. Choose the Properties option in the menu that pops up. A floating Properties window will appear. Select the Text tab in this window. Here you can do a whole bunch of styling to your title text. You can alter the font, size, colour and so on for the text. Note that this is your title text, so make it clear and big.

PDF tools
Here comes the fun bit – forms. Scribus has a number of special buttons and boxes for PDFs that we can use for this. These are part of the PDF tools kit. To make sure you can see these tools, go to Window in the menu and make sure that the PDF Tools option is checked. You should be able to see the PDF tools buttons in the menu.

Add a form
Expand the PDF Tools buttons and click on the Text Field button. Your cursor's appearance should change. Now click, drag and draw a text box next to the Name text box. Make it long enough so that a first and last name can fit in. Right-click on the newly created box and navigate to the item PDF Options. Here make sure that the option 'is PDF Annotation' is checked. Go back to the PDF Options in the right-click menu and click on Field Properties. This will pop open the Field Properties configuration window for this text box.

Configure
In the Field Properties window you will see a few options at the top, and a number of tabs below that. At the top you will see a drop-down; make sure that Text Field is the selected option here. Give your text box a name such as 'Name'. This is important, because if you later on decide to add some PHP code to your PDF, you

will refer to this item in your code by this name. Add a tooltip. Now you can tinker with the appearance of the text box and play with other options. We'll return to this bit later to add some basic form verification for our form fields.

Other fields

Repeat what you just did for the Name Text Field box for the other fields. Add ones to capture the postal address, telephone number and email address. Arrange all these boxes neatly and make sure that they all have a similar look and feel.

Add a Submit button

Now let's add a Submit button to this document and test the mailing of the captured information before we move onto the part where we work on the look of the document. At the top bar of Scribus, click on the PDF Options drop-down. Click the 'Insert PDF Push Button' button. Add a box towards the bottom of the document. Right-click on the button and go to Properties. Change the colour to something a bit bright. Add the text 'SUBMIT' to the button.

Text for Roll Over

Close the Properties window and return to the main Scribus interface. Right-click on the Submit button and launch the Field Properties for it. Give the button a name and tooltip. Under the Options tab you can add the text 'Submit' for the 'Text for Button Down', and 'Submitting your information' for the 'Text for Roll Over' fields.

Add a Reset button

Now let's add a Reset button to this document. At the top bar of Scribus, click on the PDF Options drop-down. Click the 'Insert PDF Push Button' button. Add a box towards the bottom of the document. Right-click on the button and go to Properties. Change the colour to something a bit bright. Add the text 'RESET' to the button.

Text for Roll Over

Close the Properties window and return to the main Scribus interface. Right-click on the Submit button and launch the Field Properties for it. Give the button a name and tooltip. Under the Options tab you can add the text 'Reset' for the 'Text for Button Down', and 'Resetting' for the 'Text for Roll Over' fields.

Add a Check Box

Now let's add a Check Box to this document. At the top bar of Scribus, click on the PDF Options drop-down. Click the 'Insert PDF Check Box' button. Add a box towards the bottom of the document. Right-click on the button and go to Properties. Change the colour to something a bit bright. Double Click on the Box, Give it a Name and Click on Options and Click "Default is Checked". Press OK.

Mail Action setup

Move on to the Action tab. Here we are going to configure the document to mail the information captured by the form to an email address when the user hits the Submit button. Under the Action tab, select 'Submit Form' from the Type drop-down menu.

In the 'Submit to URL' field, enter the following: 'mailto:name@address.com'. Obviously, replace this dummy email address with your own email address.

Format your document

The next option you have under the Action tab is the format in which the data should be sent. You can either have the form send you data in HTML, PDF, XFDF or FDF. We'll choose the FDF format. This is a format which is based on text, but PDF readers can use it to import data into PDF documents. Hit OK to finish the setup of the Submit button. I only have the HTML Option (Bill).

Export to PDF

You should now have a functional form document on your hands. Let's export it as a PDF document and test its functionality. At the top of the Scribus interface you will see a button titled 'Save as PDF'. Hit that button. A 'Save As PDF' window will pop up. Pick a location and filename for your document. Scribus might pop up some errors; it should be okay to hit the Ignore button. Under the General tab, choose PDF 1.3 under compatibility. You don't really need to tinker with any other options. Hit Save. Your PDF form document should be ready to go.

Open the PDF

Open the PDF document you just saved using Adobe's Acrobat Reader. Acrobat Reader is available for free on Linux, Windows and the Mac. Unfortunately most other PDF readers don't seem to support the 'smart' features we worked into our PDF. (Though Foxit PDF Reader is OK) Once the document is open, enter some data into the text fields. Hit the Submit button when done. Acrobat Reader will now either ask you if you want to send the data by email using the installed client or using a web client. At this point, pick the option you prefer. If you choose the web client option, the data you entered will be saved into an FDF file on your local hard drive. However, if you choose the email client option, a mail containing the FDF file attachment will be launched and you can hit the Send button to send the data to the email address programmed into the PDF document.

Form validation

Now that we have covered functionality, we can look at making our PDF document smarter and prettier. Let's add some basic form validation to it. Using form validation, we will have the document check the user's input to make sure they don't leave any important fields such as Name and Email Address empty. Right-click on the form next to the Name tab. Go to Field Properties. Select the Validate tab and choose the 'Custom validate script' option. Hit Edit and enter the code shown Below. Go to File > Save and Exit, then hit the OK button. Do this for the Email Address box as well. Export the document once again and test the validation.

```
if (event.value !="") {
                              app.alert("Please Complete")
}
```

Pretty up your document
Now that you have a functional document with some basic form validation, you can spend some extra time on making it look a bit nicer. Throw in a nice background colour, a couple of images such as your logo, and format the field tags with a nice-looking font and colour. To insert an image, go to Insert > Image Frame in the main menu. In a little time you should have a form document on your hands which is also easy on the eye.

Send the document
Once you are done with all of the above, export a final copy of the document as a PDF and email the document to your clients. Once they receive it and fill it out and hit the Submit button, the data they entered will be sent back to you by email. You can use Acrobat Reader to read this data or even import it directly into a spreadsheet application. Export the document once again and you're in business.

Conclusion
It works properly in Adobe Acrobat Reader or Foxit PDF Reader in Windows and Linux. I am running Linux Kubuntu 10.04.

I can Complete and Email the Form fine in Adobe Reader and Email it.

When I open the Smart PDF in a program other than Adobe Reader (Ockular), I Click "Show Forms" and then I am Able to Complete My Details. Then I can Print as a PDF (or Post Script) and then I could email that. I can also go File > Save As > Give the PDF file a New Name > Email as an Attachment. So these are a work round.

Another way is to Complete the Form in Adobe Reader or similar and then Go File > Save as Text > give it a name.txt and locate a Folder to put it in. Now create an Email and Attach the Text File.

This the Information I get via an email attachment in Linux.
Address=New+Zealand&Comments=Works+a+Treat&DTPBook=Yes&DTPCD=Ye
s&Email=leftfieldnz%40gmail.com&Phone=&name=Bill+Rosoman&Submit=

This is the .FDF file I got Back in Windows.
%FDF-1.2
1 0 obj
<</FDF <</F (/C/WINDOWS/Temporary Internet
Files/Content.IE5/EJA74X6F/creativekiwis.pdf)/Fields [<</T (Books)/V /Yes
>><</T (Email)/V (clock@slingshot.co.nz)>><</T (Course)/V /Yes >><</T
(Phone)/V (06 8674312)>><</T (name)/V (Craig Lock)>><</T (DTPCD)/V /Yes
>><</T (Address)/V (2 Elm St)>><</T (DTPBook)/V /Yes >><</T (Comments)/V
(very nice. easy and simple to complete. Lets se what happens)>>]>>>>endobj

trailer

<</Root 1 0 R>>
%%EOF

The Windows version allowed me to open the original PDF file and the Data Appeared in the Correct Fields. Very Good!

Software available at

http://www.foxitsoftware.com/downloads/index.php
http://get.adobe.com/reader/

Or all the required software for Windows and Examples and Tutorials are Available on Our Ultimate Desktop Publishing CD. See elsewhere in the Book for Details. www.creativekiwis.com/dtp.html

BTW
You may notice the Smart Form on the next page is not the actual Smart Form Document.

The reason is that it gave me some grief when I tried to upload the PDF file to Lulu.com for Printing.

The PDF contained two fonts (Helvetica and Zapfdingbats) These are old Windows fonts and especially Helvetica are not free.

Rather than spend time figure it out I deleted the page and added as normal text.

If I used it as a Smart PDF Form it would normally not matter.

The Actual Smart PDF Form is at;
www.creativekiwis.com/docs/creativekiwis.pdf

I was able to find a free copy of Zapfdingbats Font Online, but Helvetica was only available for purchase,

I will include the fonts in the CD available for this Book.

**Please Complete and Submit this Form.**

Creative Kiwis Desktop Publishing, Books, Online Courses, CDs etc.

For more information Please Complete and Submit this Form and we will get straight back to you.

This is a Smart PDF Document, You can Complete the Details and then Email it, Or Complete the Details and Print as a PDF and then Email that Document.

* Required Field

www.creativekiwis.com

Name: *

Address:

Telephone:

Email: *

Comments:

Information on Our Desktop Publishing Book:

Information on Our Desktop Publishing CD:

Information on Our Books:

Information on Our Creative Writing and Book Publishing Course:

Or Email to
leftfieldnz@gmail.com
For further Information Go To:

www.creativekiwis.com

SUBMIT RESET

## Creativekiwis.com

## Product List

==============

We have a Great Range of Products for Purchase at
www.creativekiwis.com

The Ultimate Desktop Publishing Book
==============================

Desktop Publishing using Free Open Source Software.

A Brilliant Book giving You All the Tools and Examples You Need to Create That Masterpiece within You.

Creating and publishing a magazine, books, posters, flyers, calendar, menu, award certificates, or business cards could Never Be Easier.

By Bill Rosoman Dip CS
www.lulu.com/leftfieldnz

The Ultimate Desktop Publishing CD
=============================

The CD Contains all the Software, Resources and Information You Need to Write and Publish a Book, Produce a Newspaper or Brochure.

All You Need is the Time and Inspiration!

All the tools and resources you need for creating and publishing a magazine, books, posters, flyers, calendar, menu, or business cards

The CD Contains;

* All The Necessary Windows Software
* Scribus — Desktop Publishing
* Gimp — Graphics, Pictures
* Inkscape — Vector Graphics
* Open Office — Wordprocessor etc.
* Ghostscript — Postscript Stuff
* PDF creator
* LittleCMS Colour Management System
* Calibre E-Book Reader/Converter

* Cross platform (Windows, Linux, Mac)
* All this software is free and legal

It also Includes some extra fonts.

* Some Sample Templates
* Some Howtos and Tutorials
* Some Free E-Books
* Access to Our How to Get Published Book
* Access to Our How to Get Published Course
* Access to Our How we can help You Get Published

By Bill Rosoman Dip CS
www.creativekiwis.com/dtp.html

The Simple On The Road Cook Book
================================

A Useful Easy, Simple and Budget Conscious Guide for Bachelors and other Food Preparation and Cooking Challenged People.

Especially if Living in a Confined Space or On The Road.

By Bill Rosoman Dip CS
www.lulu.com/leftfieldnz

Howto for Windows and Internet Virgins
======================================

The Basics in Using a Windows Computer. Protection, Maintenance, Programs and their Use, etc. Using Windows XP, Vista and 7. Also how the Internet works and how you can use the Internet.

Description:
A Howto for Windows and Internet Virgins. using the Windows Operating System. A Beginners Guide to using Windows.

Keywords:
howto, handbook, manual, Users Handbook, Virus Free, Operating Manual, open source software, free software, operating system, Windows XP VISTA 7, FOSS

by Bill Rosoman Dip CS
www.lulu.com/leftfieldnz

Small Business Spreadsheets CD
==============================

This is a series of simple and basic spreadsheets to help run your Home or Business effectively.

The Small Business Spreadsheets are designed to give New or Novice Computer Users essential tools required to get the most out of their computer and

Spreadsheets. And to do their accounts, GST returns, budgets, IRD returns etc. The CD has over 20 Spreadsheets. See below for details.

The CD includes Free Post and Packaging.

| | |
|---|---|
| assets.xls | Lists all your Business Assets and Calculate Depreciation |
| budget.xls | A Budget Spreadsheet |
| basiccashbook.xls | A basic one page Cash Book for a small business/home |
| cashup | A Daily Takings Record |
| contacts.xls | A List of Contacts |
| profloss.xls | Profit and Loss Spreadsheet |
| reconcil.xls | Reconcile you Bank Statement |
| gst.xls | Calculate GST Tax (for NZ) |
| ir10 | IRD form 10 |
| payment | Payment Advice |
| purchase | Purchase Order |
| receipt | Receipt |
| till | Till Take |
| trailbalance | Trail Balance |
| yearbudget | Yearly Budget |
| fuelconsume.xls | Calculate Fuel Consumption |
| paysummary.xls | Summary of Pay |
| purchase.xls | Purchase Order |
| receipt.xls | Receipt |
| theaccounts.doc | Document and How To for Spreadsheets |
| time.xls | Time Sheet |
| wages.xls | Wages |
| yearbudget.xls | Year Budget |

The CD includes a comprehensive Manual on using the Business Spreadsheets.

by Bill Rosoman Dip CS
www.creativekiwis.com/spreadsheets.html

Creative Writing and Book Publishing Course
=======================================

The Creative Writing and Book Publishing Course.

Get Cracking and get your book written, completed and published now!

We offer the complete package of helping you write that book within you and to get it published.

The Course is fifteen lessons via email with an input from your Personal Tutors.

At the end of the course you will have a published book, if you have a manuscript ready to go!
www.creativekiwis.com

Angolan Dawn
===========

A Novel by prolific Author Craig Lock.

A true tale of an Angolan migrant miner who goes to 'e'Goli', the big city of gold in South Africa.

Also a realistic portrayal of the Angolan conflict in "darkest Africa" through the eyes of a hospital orderly.

A moving and realistic novel about the evil and destructiveness of war, as well as the inherent goodness within every human spirit.

Keywords: History, Angola, Southern Africa, Legacy, Gisborne, New Zealand, South Africa, Travel, Africa, War, Politics, Humanity, Conflict, Novel

By Craig Lock
www.lulu.com/clock

How to Write a Book and Get Published
(ALL THAT I KNOW ABOUT WRITING!)
===================================

Authors Craig Lock and Bill Rosoman

Get Cracking and get your book written, completed and published now!

We offer the complete package of helping you write that book within you and to get it published. At the end of the book you will have a published book, if you have a manuscript ready to go!

By Craig Lock
www.lulu.com/clock

Over the Rainbow
==============

A look at the many colourful peoples, who make up this diverse and vibrant society, as seen through the eyes of a newspaper reporter. Many colourful "vignettes" in this "land of great contrasts" - happy, sad and true, that was the fabric of South African life in the lead up to the historic Democratic Election of 1994.

We live in a very complex country of great disparities and extremes, especially in wealth and in living standards. A land of great contradictions: a land of sunshine, a world in one country, a land of laughter in this strange and beautiful place. Much of the laughter from the very people, who have suffered the most and felt the most pain in this strange tormented place of ours. Yes, there is that sadness in the eyes of them too.

So to put it simply, South Africa is just one happy, sad land...and I hope that the lives of ALL South Africans will become better in the days ahead

By Craig Lock
www.lulu.com/clock

The New Rainbow
==============

A tale of the many people in the rainbow nation of New South Africans.

By Craig Lock
www.lulu.com/clock

Creative Writing Course
===================

Available Online Now for you to complete by email at your leisure.

Ever wanted to write? A short story or perhaps even a book? Is there a talent for creative writing within you? How do you know if there is? Do you have some interesting experiences to share, your life story perhaps?
We have Creative Writing Course for you, it may provide that spark to get you into print and to publish that book lurking inside you!

There is a vast market of readers out there expectantly waiting for new information, insights and experiences - real people with whom you could share many interesting subjects. They might want to hear about your experiences, your thoughts, your unique ideas, and even perhaps the tale of your life...because I believe that everyone has some story within them just waiting to be told and shared.

So open up your inner world to them through creative writing. Unleash those creative talents within you.

This is your chance to begin.

By Craig Lock
www.creativekiwis.com

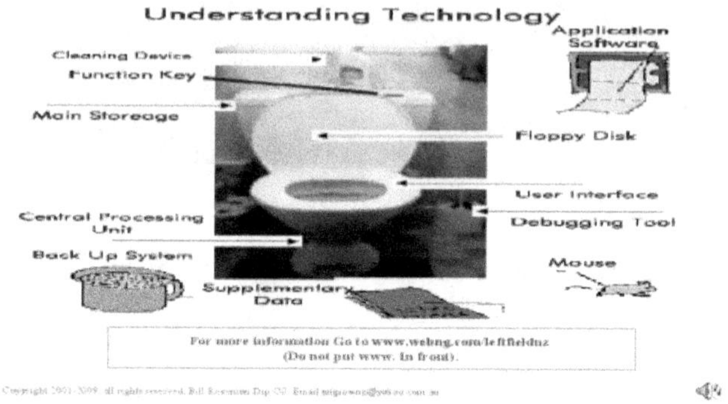
Understanding Technology
Application Software
Cleaning Device
Function Key
Main Storeage
Floppy Disk
User Interface
Central Processing Unit
Debugging Tool
Back Up System
Mouse
Supplementary Data
For more information Go to www.webng.com/leftfieldnz
(Do not put www. In front).

Small Business Spreadsheets CD
Nugrow Technologies and
Eagle Productions 2008
www.webng.com/leftfieldnz
© Copyright 2008
All rights Reserved

THE NEW RAINBOW
CRAIG LOCK

# The Ultimate Desktop Publishing Book Conclusions

It has been a lot of fun and a massive learning curve to create this book.

I sincerely hope you find the book and CD useful.

I am particularly impressed with Scribus.
Scribus does a great job especially with PDF Smart Forms and Embedded Fonts. It does not do Web Addresses you can click through on but that is the only negative I have found.

The only thing with Scribus is to remember that it is not a Word Processor Program. Do most of your Text in MS Word or Open Office Writer and Save As Unformatted Text.

I also found using The Gimp for Photos and Inkscape for Vector Graphics great and they did the job required of them.

Another great find was Calibre an E-Book Reader and Converter. It is great for reading PDF and EPUB books and to converting them for Kindle, Nook, Ipod etc. It will also Download Free Newspapers and Magazines which is a Wonderful Feature.

I started this book when a Lady gave a talk on Desktop Publishing at the local Computer Club. She uses Windows and about $1500 of software mainly from Adobe. Though I think she said she paid a Student Rate for her software. While that is great and her choice, I only use Kubuntu Linux and Not Windows and believe that the best things in life are free and you should not have to pay for software to do a good job.

So over all the process of writng a book, doing a flyer or brochure is certainly enhanced by the use of the suggested software in this book.

May I recommend
http://wiki.scribus.net/index.php and http://docs.scribus.net/

as good sources of information

BTW if you are doing the same project often, then save a copy of the outline of your project as a Template, that will save a lot of time and effort.

To Save As PDF/X-3
Edit > Preferences > Color Management make sure color management is enabled
Save as PDF
Under PDF/X-3
Put Book Title as Info String

As mentioned elsewhere be careful of the fonts you use, make sure they are TTF True Type Fonts. Test by Opening in PDF Reader and Going To, File > Properties > Fonts.

I would be real careful and only use a few fonts and then check that they appear embedded in the PDF Document, or you will have trouble printing the result.

Times New Roman is the Classic Desktop Publishing Font so the most Useful.

**Notes**

# Notes

**The Ultimate Desktop Publishing Book**

by
Bill Rosoman Dip CS


Bill Rosoman leftfieldnz@gmail.com

Published by
Bill Rosoman Dip CS

layout and Design by www.lulu.com

Printed by www.lulu.com

Copies of this book can be ordered from
www.lulu.com/leftfieldnz

or
Bill Rosoman
PO Box 4155
Hamilton East 3247
New Zealand

ISBN 978-0-473-17409-5

www.ingramcontent.com/pod-product-compliance
Lightning Source LLC
LaVergne TN
LVHW060455061126
851857LV00016B/1841
* 9 7 8 0 4 7 3 1 7 4 0 9 5 *